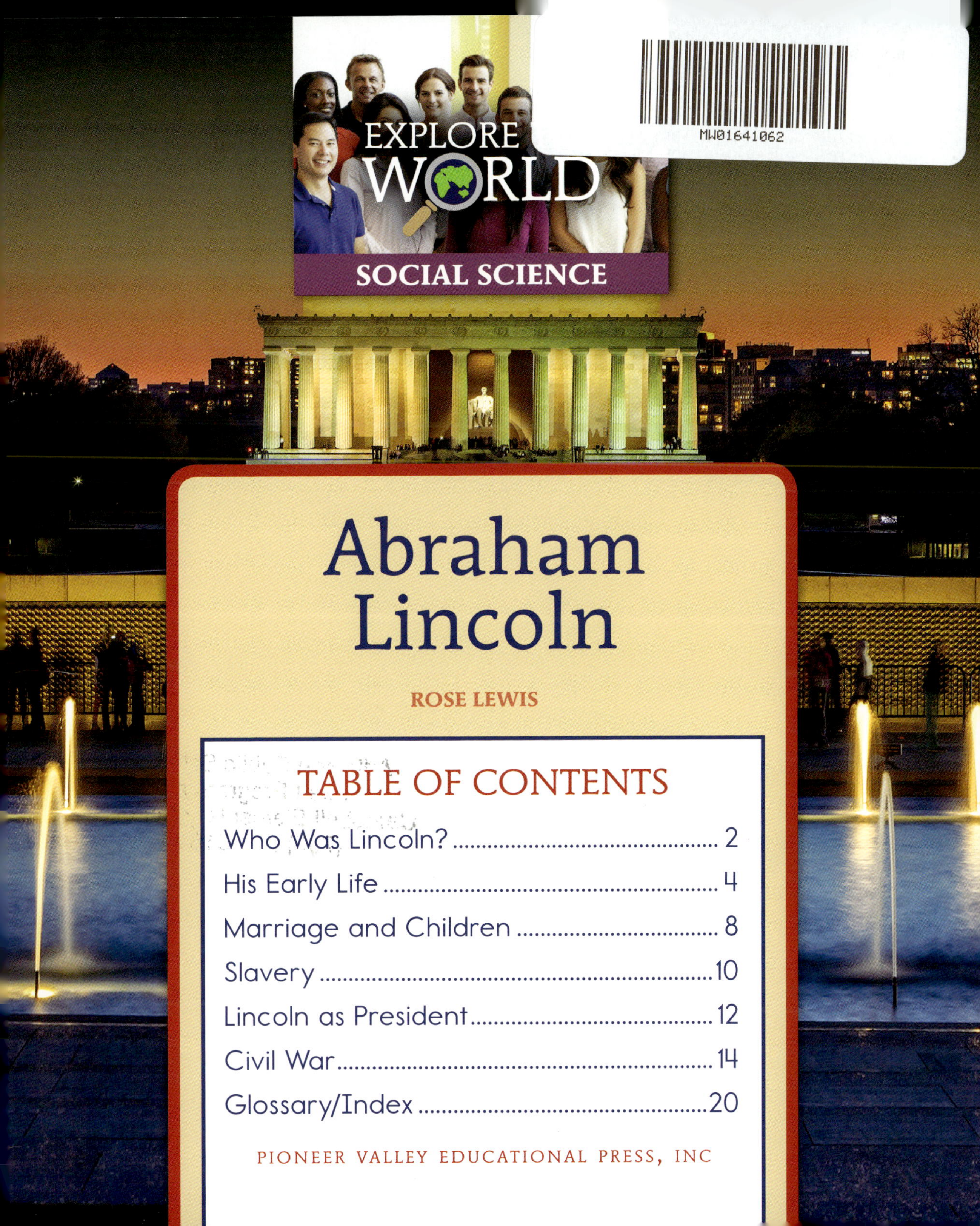

Abraham Lincoln

ROSE LEWIS

TABLE OF CONTENTS

Who Was Lincoln? 2
His Early Life 4
Marriage and Children 8
Slavery 10
Lincoln as President 12
Civil War 14
Glossary/Index 20

PIONEER VALLEY EDUCATIONAL PRESS, INC

WHO WAS LINCOLN?

Abraham Lincoln was one of the most famous **presidents** of the United States. He helped free the **slaves.**

HIS EARLY LIFE

Abraham Lincoln was born
in a log **cabin**.
The cabin was very small.
It had only one room.

When Abraham was
just nine years old,
his mother died.
His sister took care of him.
Then Abraham's father
got married again.

When Abraham was seven, his family moved to a place where there was no school.

Abraham loved to read. He would walk a long way to get a book from a friend.

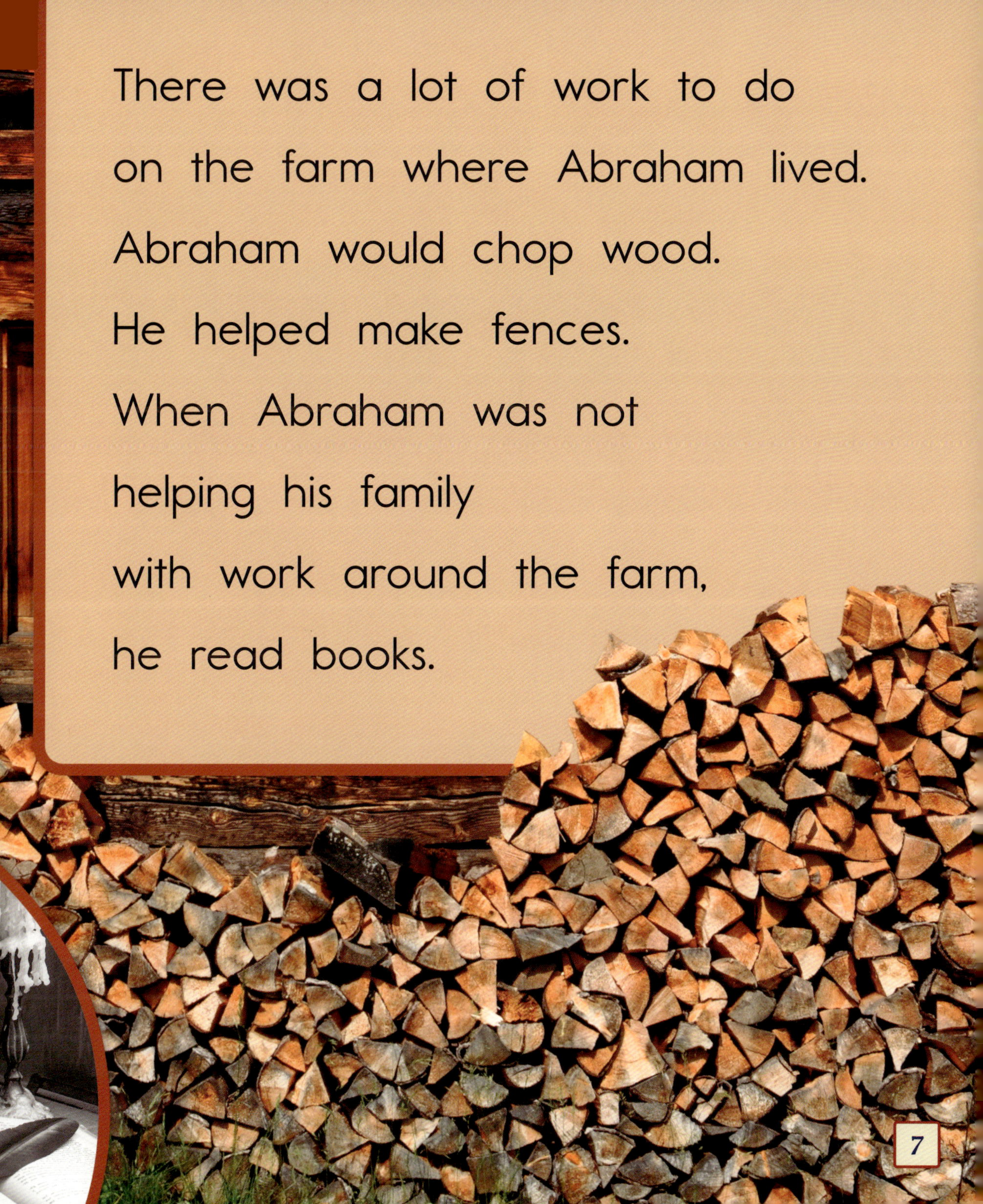

There was a lot of work to do on the farm where Abraham lived. Abraham would chop wood. He helped make fences. When Abraham was not helping his family with work around the farm, he read books.

MARRIAGE AND CHILDREN

Abraham Lincoln married Mary Todd.

Abraham and Mary had four children. Three of their children died. This made both Mary and Abraham very sad.

Abraham read books to learn about the law. He became a lawyer.

SLAVERY

Some farmers had slaves working in their fields. Abraham Lincoln did not like that people had slaves. He did not think anyone should be a slave. He made speeches against **slavery**.

MORE TO EXPLORE

Many black people from Africa were brought to the United States to be slaves. They worked on farms.

MORE TO EXPLORE

Some people helped slaves escape from slavery. People helped hide slaves as they traveled north. The route was called the **UNDERGROUND RAILROAD**.

LINCOLN AS PRESIDENT

On November 6, 1860, Abraham Lincoln was **elected** president of the United States. Many people in the South did not vote for Lincoln. They did not want him to be president.

This was the United States' flag at the time of the Civil War.

People in the South
did not want
to be part of the United States
of America any longer.
They wanted to be a new country.

The people in the South made a new flag for their country.

CIVIL WAR

A war began.
The people in the South
were fighting
the people in the North.

Lincoln wanted slaves

to be free.

He made a speech saying

that all slaves were free.

There were many years of fighting during the Civil War.

Many men died.

Men from the South died and men from the North died, too.

Finally, after four long years, the war was over. The North won the war. The North and South were back together. The slaves were also free.

On April 14, 1865,
when Lincoln was watching a play,
he was shot.
He died the next day.

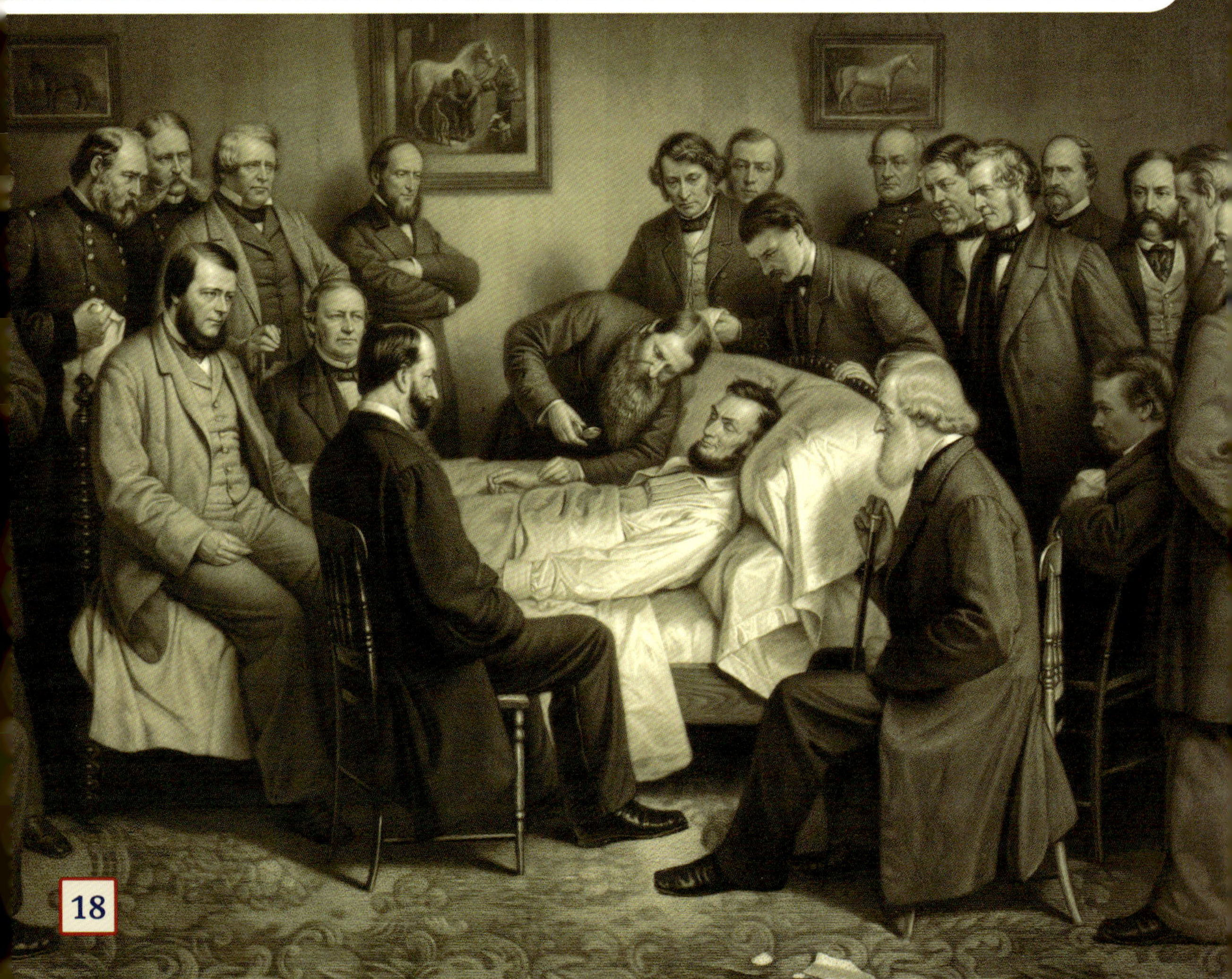

GLOSSARY

cabin
small house made of wood

elected
to choose someone by voting

president
person who leads the country

slave
a person who is owned by another person and must work without pay

slavery
to keep slaves

INDEX

books 6–7
cabin 4
civil war 14–15, 16–17
elected 12
farm 7
lawyer 8
married 4, 8
Mary Todd 8
North 14, 16–17
president 2, 12
school 6
slavery 10–11
slaves 2, 10–11, 15, 19
South 12–13, 14, 16–17
speeches 10–11, 15
Underground Railroad 11

ABRAHAM LINC

1809

Lincoln is born in a log cabin on February 12.

1842

Lincoln marries Mary Todd.

1860

Lincoln is elected the 16th president of the United States.

1861

The Civil War begins.

COLN TIME LINE

Address delivered at the dedication of the Cemetery at Gettysburg.

Four score and seven years ago our fathers brought forth on this continent, a new nation, conceived in Liberty, and dedicated to the proposition that all men are created equal.

Now we are engaged in a great civil war, testing whether that nation, or any nation so conceived and so dedicated, can long endure. We are met on a great battle-field of that war. We have come to dedicate a portion of that field, as a final resting place for those who here gave their lives, that that nation might live. It is altogether fitting and proper that we should do this.

But, in a larger sense, we can not dedicate— we can not consecrate— we can not hallow— this ground. The brave men, living and dead, who struggled here, have consecrated it, far above our poor power to add

1863

Lincoln makes a speech freeing the slaves on January 1.

1865

The Civil war ends on April 9.

1865

Lincoln dies after he is shot by John Wilkes Booth on April 15.

Today, Abraham Lincoln is remembered because he helped free the slaves.

You can visit the Lincoln Memorial in Washington, D.C.